What are FRIENDS FOR?

**FIRST PUBLISHED IN 2009
BY CONARI PRESS,**

an imprint of

RED WHEEL/WEISER, LLC

With offices at:

**500 Third Street, Suite 230
San Francisco, CA 94107**
www.redwheelweiser.com

Grateful acknowledgement is made to BJ Gallagher for permission to quote her briefly in these pages.

ISBN: 978-1-57324-414-5

Library of Congress
Cataloging-in-Publication Data
available upon request.

COVER AND TEXT DESIGN
by Tracy Sunrize Johnson

TYPESET IN Cheltenham, Stymie, Futura, Hoefler Text, Gotham, Signpainter, League Night, and Wendy

Printed in Hong Kong

SS

10 9 8 7 6 5 4 3 2 1

What are

FRIENDS

FOR?

MARSHA KARZMER

Conari Press

Contents

FRIENDS

What are friends for?

My hunch is, you already know – that's why you're reading this book. Friends are for listening with love, sharing our struggles, and helping from the heart. Friends are for talking together, laughing together, adventuring through life together.

The colorful book you hold in your hands is remarkable for asking such a warm, inviting question. It is also remarkable in that it was "written" entirely by assembling bits and pieces from women's magazines—headlines from articles, phrases from ads, quips and quotes from sidebars. Marsha Karzmer takes the words of many women, from many sources, and assembles them in wonderful books. In a sense, then, these are the words of Everywoman.

And yet Marsha's own lyrical voice comes through crystal clear. Her sense of fun, her ability to find humor in the mundane, and her zest for life all animate the clips and quotes on these pages.

Conari designers have taken Marsha's "clip notes" and given them a look that can only be described as yummy eye candy! With its sumptuous colors, textures, graphics, and design, this lovely book is the perfect gift for girlfriends, sisters, moms, aunts, and any other important women in your life. This book tells them that they are your cherished friends — forever!

— BJ GALLAGHER, *author of*

Everything I Need to Know I Learned from Other Women

FOREWORD

Time passes, life happens, distance separates, children
grow up, jobs come and go.

LOVE WAXES AND WANES.

Men don't do what they're supposed to do.

Hearts break.

Parents die.

COLLEAGUES FORGET FAVORS.

Careers end.

BUT...

A girlfriend is never farther away than needing her can reach.
When you have to walk that lonesome valley and you have to walk it
By yourself, the women in your life will be on the valley's rim,
Cheering you on, praying for you, pulling for you, intervening on
Your behalf, and waiting with open arms at the valley's end.

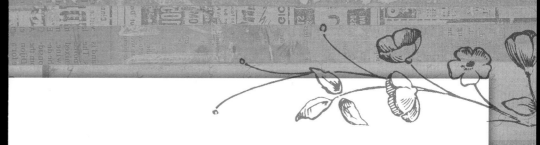

Sometimes, they will even break the rules and walk beside you.
Or come in and carry you out—
Girlfriends, daughters, granddaughters, daughters-in-law, sisters,
Sisters-in-law, mothers, grandmothers, aunties, nieces, cousins, and
The extended family, all bless our life!
The world wouldn't be the same without women, and neither would I.
When we began this adventure called womanhood, we had no idea of
The incredible joys our sorrows that lay ahead. Nor did we know how
Much we would need each other.
We need each other still.

—an email fwded to me by a girlfriend,
fwded to her by a girlfriend
and on and on and on . . .

FRIENDS

heavy
mole-
c. to

———

It is intended that a

A big turkey shoot

INSPIRE
YOU

friends

teach you that

EVERYONE YOU MEET HAS A LESSON FOR YOU

and everyone you deal with

may be your teacher.

...MAKE YOU *laugh.*

MAKE YOU **CRY.**

MAKE YOU reflect.

. . . **are weird.**

But a good kind of weird.

THEY WON'T LET YOU DOWN.

. . . LET YOU SHOW THEM YOUR DREAMS.

YOU YOUR FRIENDS

because they are

UNEDITED.

UNPREDICTABLE.

Unforgettable.

HOW WILL SHE SURPRISE US NEXT?

FRIENDS

help you feel

fearless and fabulous

AND

START ACCENTUATING THE POSITIVE.

. . . won't let you be less than your best,

EVEN IF YOU SOMETIMES WANT TO KICK HER.

. . . have a better understanding of life, living, and loving.

ISN'T THIS
THE BEST GIFT
YOU'VE EVER RECEIVED
FROM A WOMAN?

Be a phenomenal woman.

IT'S NOT A MATTER OF

how far we've come,

BUT

HOW FAR WE'RE GOING.

Could you use a little inspiration?

A BIT OF OPTIMISM,

A SPIRITUALITY CHECK,

A LITTLE SOUND ADVICE?

An understanding friend is better than a therapist;

AND CHEAPER TOO!

 So balance your life the wisdom of a few good women.

FRIENDS

It is intended that a

A big turkey

Hang Out With You

WHEN WAS THE LAST TIME YOU WERE ABLE TO

slip out the door

to meet your friends

 *hang with the girls?*

Friendship has its

REWARDS.

Friends GIVE YOU

A GIFT OF LAUGHTER

and

something to think about.

Sometimes you don't have to say a word.

Friends

DO THE
UNEXPECTED.

One friend told me,

> **" I love ice cream so much
> that I can't imagine life without it. "**

Another said,

> *" Any dessert that doesn't have chocolate
> is a pointless dessert. "*

...and of course,

THEY TALK ABOUT

Friends

DRAG OUT OF YOU

all the details

YOU'RE SECRETLY DYING TO SHARE.

MY IDEA OF A GREAT DAY

 is

shopping with my girlfriends.

Shopping allows you to say to me,

"I don't think Paul is the right guy for you," or

"I think you should go back into therapy—

ooh!—what do you think of this shirt?"

Where would I be if it weren't for my women friends?

We laugh together, cry together, compare notes on our children, and complain about our jobs.

We do lunch, we go shopping, we borrow each other's clothes.

It's all about the miracles that can happen when friends connect to

HAVE SOME FUN

share some snacks

AND CHANGE THE WORLD.

FRIENDS

NO. B

It is intended that a

PROVIDE A SHOULDER

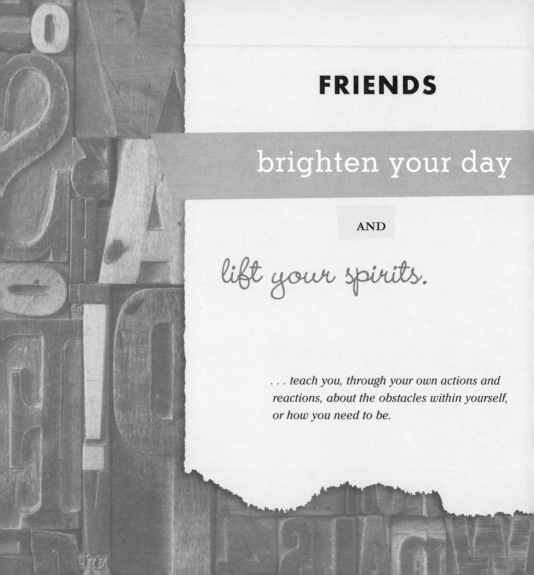

FRIENDS

brighten your day

AND

lift your spirits.

. . . teach you, through your own actions and reactions, about the obstacles within yourself, or how you need to be.

THERE IS SOMETHING SO

ESSENTIAL AND PRIMORDIAL

in women sharing with other women.

It seems the most natural thing in the world.

Give me the support of a few good women friends,
and I can do almost anything!

She may tell you

WHAT TO SAY TO INCONSIDERATE NEIGHBORS

AND HOW TO

eat breakfast on the run

and then

DE-STRESS AT YOUR DESK.

. . . how to de-clutter your life

AND HOW TO

get organized,

STAVE OFF STRESS.

Even if you don't have a reason to call or email me,

GO AHEAD!

YOU CAN CALL ANYTIME!

No kidding!

SOMEONE ONCE SAID THAT

the good part about helping a friend in need

is that it shows you

your finest self.

I'LL BE THERE WHEN YOU NEED ME.

I depend on you for so much—

COMPANY, COMFORT, GUIDANCE, ADVICE,

and sometimes

a good swift kick when I need it!

I AM SO GLAD YOU'RE HERE.

FRIENDS

NO. 18

enavy
nole-
c. to

It is intended that a

A big turkey shoot will be

Tell You the Truth

Friends

EQUAL

no fake smiles.

NO HIDDEN AGENDAS.

NO BULL.

Friends know how to talk politics and still stay friends.

She may tell you

lighten up.

GET A LIFE.

... think less.

Dream more.

A GOOD FRIEND WILL ALWAYS TELL YOU

THE GOOD,

THE BAD,

AND THE

... no, honey you can't wear Lycra anymore.

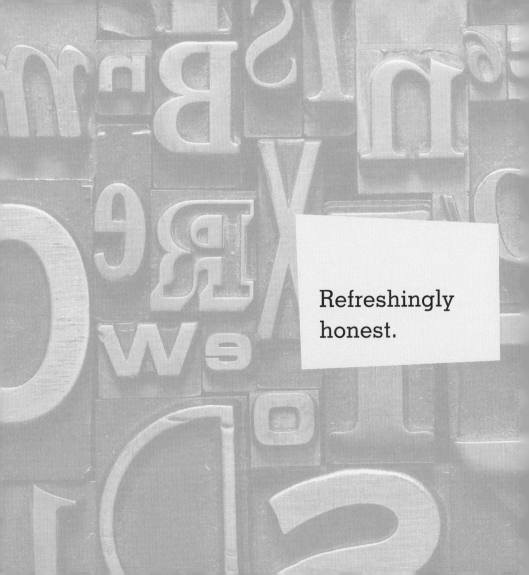

Refreshingly
honest.

 **what** do women

secretly say

WHEN THEY ARE TALKING

to a friend?

These are things wish they knew,

but if they did they would have to

SEEK PROFESSIONAL HELP

immediately

THEY WON'T BE TALKING ABOUT THE WEATHER.

or

**SPRING
CLEANING!**

Each time my friend tells a story, it's

IRRESISTIBLE

illicit

AND SOMETIMES IT'S EVEN TRUE.

We talk about the mistakes she made with her kids,

the best kind of face-lift,

her crazy little hair secret.

WE REALLY, REALLY DO.

And it gets worse.

We also talk about
what kind of
tree
Diane Sawyer would be.

Just the other day I told my friend,

 We're such good friends,

if I got invited to a

BIG HOLLYWOOD PARTY ,

I'd call you the minute I got home.

Or if you had stuff on your face,

I'd tell you,

sooner or later. "

Independent.

EVER CHANGING.

Constantly surprising.

Friends have

**THE SMALL ANSWERS
TO LIFE'S BIG QUESTIONS**

and will tell you

THE GOOD,

THE BAD,

and . . . the funny.

FRIENDS

It is intended that a

A big turkey shoot

**REMIND YOU
OF WHO YOU CAN BE**

FRIENDS

HELP YOU

STAND FOR SOMETHING
AND BE COMFORTABLE DOING IT.

...make you realize that

there is more to life than just you.

. . . CAN TEACH YOU HOW TO

kick up your aura

AND

SHOW YOUR TRUE COLORS.

. . . remind you the only person you need to be is

yourself.

We are different in our goals

BUT NOT SO DIFFERENT

in what we give up

to reach them.

FRIENDS

help you stay

FIT, sane, *and*

ON TOP OF YOUR GAME.

A friend won't let you be less than your best,

EVEN IF YOU SOMETIMES WANT TO KICK HER.

We're in great physical shape these days, but now we need to stretch our nerve as well as our quads, firm up our guts as well as our tummies.

THERE ARE SOME THINGS
EVEN THE BEST SCHOOLS
CAN'T TEACH YOU.

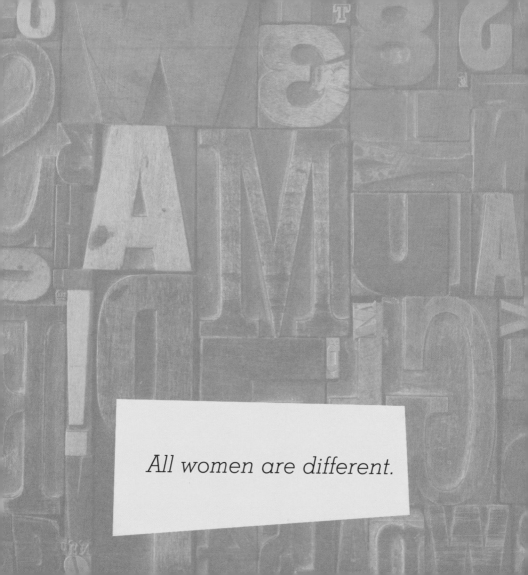

All women are different.

WE NURTURE ONE ANOTHER.

And we need to have

UNPRESSURED SPACE

IN WHICH WE CAN DO

the special kind of talk that women do

when they're with other women.

It's a very healing experience.

Being friends is like being

different pieces of the same puzzle.

FRIENDS

heavy
mole-
ic. to

It is intended that a

NO. 11

A big turkey shoot

m

HELP YOU LIVE IT UP

FRIENDS *can show you how to get*

MORE FUN

in your life.

ONE WAY TO

break the monotony of everyday life

is

get some friendship therapy.

FRIENDS WILL TAKE YOU

OUT FOR COCKTAILS

to celebrate life

and

the holidays.

IT'S ALL ABOUT

WINE,

women,

and

WHAT TO DRINK WITH PUMPKIN PIE.

Dishing with the girls.

Mmm, delicious!

STEAMY.

SIZZLING.

SEDUCTIVE. *And that was just the weather.*

TRAVEL IN THE COMPANY OF STARS.

We are *bodacious*

and

OUTRAGEOUS

and

rad.

VIXEN VIGILANTES,

vamping viragoes

otherwise very nice women.

It's party time—

TIME TO PULL OUT THE STOPS

and

LIVE A LITTLE.

We always say we're going to

ENTERTAIN MORE

AND

celebrate our friendships.

LET'S **JUST DO IT**

!

FRIENDS

It is intended that a

heavy
mole-
c. to

A big turkey

Love You Best

Not since you lived with **MOM** *and* **DAD**

have you gotten

SO MUCH FOR SO LITTLE.

Friends

think you're

...there's no one else like you.

Friends

BELIEVE IN YOU

even when you've

CEASED TO BELIEVE

in

yourself.

. . . love us for who we are.

Is it a

PICTURE-PERFECT

friendship ?

Or what?

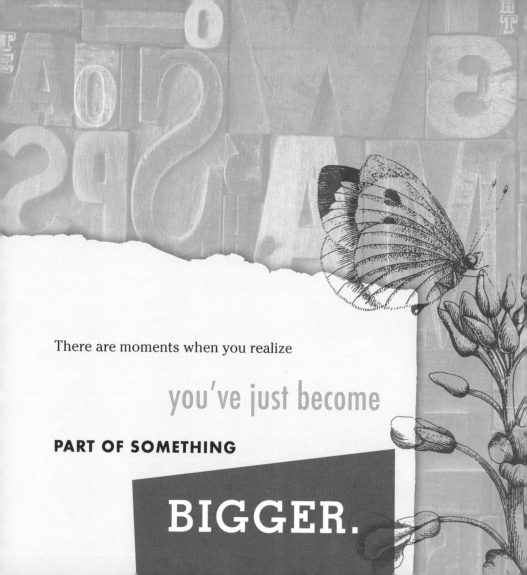

There are moments when you realize

you've just become

PART OF SOMETHING

BIGGER.

*Sow the seeds of friendship
and you will reap wisdom*

AND

live joyously.

IF YOU WANT TO KNOW HOW

to be an even better friend,

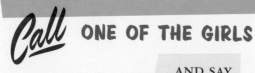

JUST PICK UP THE PHONE.

Call **ONE OF THE GIRLS**

AND SAY,

I wanted you to know that I will always be there for you: I promise you that. I will always be your friend.

What it comes down to is:

Many people will walk in and out of your life,
but only true friends will leave footprints on your heart.

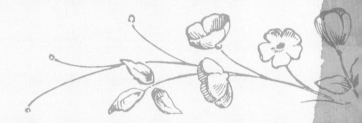

Your friends are the best;

GIVE THEM THE WORLD.

SHOW HOW YOU LOVE THEM!

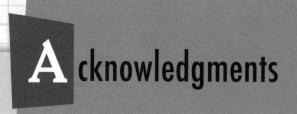

Acknowledgments

To all the

Wonderful Women

in my life.
I promise to always be there for you.

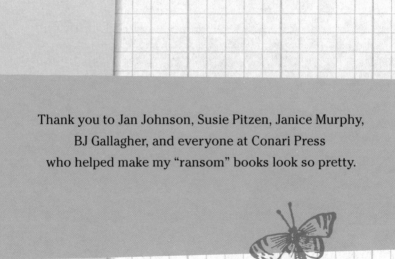

Thank you to Jan Johnson, Susie Pitzen, Janice Murphy,
BJ Gallagher, and everyone at Conari Press
who helped make my "ransom" books look so pretty.

T o

OUR READERS

CONARI PRESS, an imprint of **RED WHEEL/WEISER,** publishes books on topics ranging from spirituality, personal growth, and relationships to women's issues, parenting, and social issues. Our mission is to publish quality books that will make a difference in people's lives—how we feel about ourselves and how we relate to one another. We value integrity, compassion, and receptivity, both in the books we publish and in the way we do business.

Our readers are our most important resource, and we value your input, suggestions, and ideas about what you would like to see published. Please feel free to contact us, to request our latest book catalog, or to be added to our mailing list.

CONARI PRESS

An imprint of

RED WHEEL/WEISER, LLC

500 Third Street, Suite 230
San Francisco, CA 94107
www.redwheelweiser.com